Original title:
Field of Vision

Copyright © 2025 Creative Arts Management OÜ
All rights reserved.

Author: Oliver Bennett
ISBN HARDBACK: 978-1-80567-044-5
ISBN PAPERBACK: 978-1-80567-124-4

The Visionary Path

On a path where wobbly thoughts reside,
I tripped on a rock, my brain took a ride.
A squirrel gave me tips on how to go slow,
While birds debated snacks, oh what a show!

I followed a butterfly, thought it was wise,
But it led me in circles, oh what a surprise!
A frog in a tuxedo gave me a grin,
Said, "Life is a party, come join in the spin!"

Windows to the Infinite

From my window, I spotted a cat in a hat,
Dancing with shadows, how silly is that?
The trees held a meeting, discussing the breeze,
While grass blades giggled, doing little sneezes.

I peered through the glass, saw clouds in a race,
Competing for space, oh what a wild chase!
A raindrop declared it was king of the day,
As puddles all cheered in a slippery sway!

A Journey Through the Senses

I took a deep sniff of a pie on the sill,
Turned out it was paper, my nose needs a chill.
I tasted the sunshine, a sweet, sticky mess,
Shouldn't have worn sandals—oh, what a distress!

I listened for laughter in the tick of the clock,
Only found silence, and my socks on a rock.
I touched the soft breeze, it tickled my cheek,
And danced with the daisies, so light and so meek!

Panorama of Dreams

In a dream, I flew with a jellybean crew,
We soared over marshmallows, oh what a view!
A llama in pajamas offered us tea,
While cupcakes spun tales of sweet victory.

Each dream was a ride on a bubblegum cloud,
Wearing socks made of rainbows, yes, feeling proud.
So here's to the whims that our minds like to weave,
In landscapes of humor, we're free to believe!

The Architecture of Seeing

I built a house made of my thoughts,
With windows wide for peeking spots.
The doors are jokes that swing and sway,
In rooms where laughter loves to play.

Each corner holds a silly scene,
A dance of shadows, bright and keen.
But as I gaze, the walls do move,
My sight's a game, with nothing to prove.

Fragments of Clarity

I found my glasses in a drawer,
They showed me things I'd not explore.
A squirrel knitting on a tree,
Creating hats for birds and bees!

The sun wore socks, a sight most rare,
While clouds were having a morning flair.
I squinted twice, then laughed out loud,
In fragments caught, I felt so proud.

Tides of Insight

A beach of thoughts, the tide rolls in,
With waves of ideas, a toothy grin.
Seashells whisper secrets of the day,
While crabs do cha-cha in their play.

I watched as seagulls tried to surf,
Each ride a laugh, a twist, a swerve.
With every splash and sparkling sight,
My mind just danced with pure delight.

Waving Minds

Two minds met under a big tree,
They waved hello, both wild and free.
One wore a hat, the other shoes,
Their laughter echoed in vibrant hues.

Ideas floated like balloons so bright,
A juggling act of pure delight.
With every wave, they sparked a thought,
In this odd world, joy is sought.

Gazing Beyond Limits

I peered out my window too wide,
And saw my neighbor's cat on a ride.
It strutted like it owned the street,
While I laughed alone at its queenly feat.

A bird flew by with a snack in its beak,
I blinked too long, thought it would speak.
My glasses slipped down, what a silly scene,
I squinted hard; was that cat wearing green?

Light and Shadow Dance

The shadows on the wall play tricks,
They twist and turn like they're in the mix.
My lamp's gone wild, with a mind of its own,
Making shapes of a gnome who's all alone.

I chuckled at shadows that flickered and fell,
A quirky reunion, can you tell?
They danced about without a beat,
While my dog joined in, thinking it's a treat.

The Depths of Sight

My eyes explored the depths of the room,
Finding dust bunnies that look like a bloom.
They've gathered in corners, holding a ball,
Planning their heist to take over the hall.

A fly buzzed by, my main event,
I tracked its moves, my time well spent.
But it dodged my hand with a laugh and a spin,
I just wanted to ask how it got in.

Outward Bound Impressions

I stepped outside to enjoy the view,
A squirrel shot by, wearing something blue.
"Fashion choice, or just a snag?" I cried,
It winked at me and ran off to hide.

A dog strolled up, wearing sneakers so bright,
He looked me directly in the eyes with delight.
"Did I miss the memo?" I wanted to say,
As fashion trends soared in a different way.

Periphery of Knowing

I squint my eyes to find a clue,
Around me sprawls a view that's new.
My glasses thick, my sight a blur,
I trip on life, is it a spur?

What's that over there, a duck with flair?
Or just my neighbor's cat in air?
Each twist and glance reveals the jest,
I'm lost but hey, this sight's the best!

The Spectrum of Experience

Colors blast from every nook,
Did I just see a flying brook?
A rainbow sprouting from a shoe,
Now that's a shade I never knew!

Peering through the kaleidoscope,
Finding laughter helps me cope.
My glasses cracked, but what a sight,
Swinging through day, dancing with light!

Embracing the Unexplored

In shadows lurk the wackiest sights,
Like squirrels wearing hats, oh what delights!
An adventure lies just out of reach,
With every glance, the world's a peach!

Oh! A cactus dressed in a tutu spin,
Is this madness or just a win?
Exploring corners, never quite done,
Each oddity found is a new kind of fun!

The Broadening Perception

Seeing things at odd angles,
Is it truth or just some wrangles?
A penguin playing chess on ice,
And ducks that dance? Now that's not nice!

With every twist, my eyes go wide,
A marshmallow who seems to glide.
The absurdity of it all makes me grin,
In this whimsical ride, I always win!

Whispers of the Gaze

I squint and see a squirrel dance,
In shades of gray, it takes a chance.
With every leap, it seems to say,
'Why walk when you can hop and play?'

My glasses fog, I wipe the lens,
Did I just spot my neighbor's friends?
They wave and smile, what a delight,
Fish still biting, will it take flight?

A bird in blue, so sharp and bright,
Screeches loudly, gives me quite a fright.
It lands and stares, a judgmental gaze,
While I trip over my own shoelace!

With laughter shared under the sun,
We watch the world, we look for fun.
Every glance reveals the grand,
In this quirky, bustling land.

Breathing in the Light

The sun peeks through, a golden show,
Where shadows dance and rabbits glow.
I grab a hat, it's quite a sight,
To shield my eyes from the glaring light!

A butterfly flits, quite a charmer,
Looking for nectar, such a gardener!
With every scoop, it plays a prank,
While I chase it down, my breath is rank!

A distant laugh makes me look around,
It's my dog, rolling on the ground!
Chasing his tail, what a silly plight,
Shining bright, under the sunlight.

The garden blooms with colors vast,
In every glance, a memory cast.
So much to see, so much delight,
In each simple moment, breathing light.

An Odyssey of Perspectives

With a twist and a turn, I seek a view,
A pickle jar, stuck! Who knew?
I give it a tug, the lid holds tight,
A great moment, my face a bright sight!

The cat on the fence looks rather smug,
As if he's just won a cozy hug.
With a stretch and a yawn, he declines,
To notice my plight, as he reclines.

Through the window, kids play tag in the sun,
Laughter and shouts, oh what fun!
A game of chase, who will be spry?
Peeking past curtains, oh my, oh my!

Every glance tells a story untold,
In this wild world, we all feel bold.
So laugh through the chaos, never forget,
Life's funny moments are the best bet!

The Wide Angle of Thought

In the corners of my brain,
Ideas dance a silly game.
A rubber chicken, so absurd,
Cackles at the thoughts we've stirred.

A view that stretches far and wide,
With giggles as our trusty guide.
We're peering through a glass so fogged,
Yet clarity is fairly clogged.

Thoughts bump into one another,
Like kids who can't find one another.
We zoom in close, then pull away,
It's quite the wacky cabaret!

The frame expands, then it constricts,
A circus tent of wild conflicts.
Where laughter reigns and weird things sprout,
Creating visions, roundabout!

Panoramic Wishes

A wish upon a twinkling star,
At breakfast shared with cheese and tar.
A panoramic view so spry,
With jellybeans that leap and fly.

From right to left, I hear a hum,
As candy critters start to drum.
A landscape full of pure delight,
Where pickles put up quite a fight!

I wish for fries that dance at noon,
With ketchup singing silly tunes.
The sky is filled with soda spray,
A fizzy, funny, wild ballet!

So here's my wish, it's quite the hoot,
A park where laughter bears a flute.
With each deep breath, the joy unfurls,
In this wide world of wacky swirls!

The Shape of Curious Eyes

My eyes are shaped like funny pies,
With whiskers probing for good fries.
They bounce about, a curious spree,
Exploring all that they can see.

A squirrel wearing funky hats,
Perplexed by chatting acrobat cats.
Through blinking lids, the world spins bright,
As giggles turn the day to night.

Bizarre and twisted, shapes collide,
A rollercoaster curvy ride.
With every blink, a tale unfolds,
Of silly mysteries and glimmers bold.

And when I squint to spy the skies,
They shoot back winks with playful sighs.
In this strange land of curious hues,
The shape of eyes brings cheerful views!

Lattice of Understanding

In a lattice made of giggles bright,
Each thread a joke, a pure delight.
Weaving wisdom in a twist,
Where sense and nonsense both exist.

A crisscross of ideas, what a sight,
Like tangled yarn in morning light.
Every knot a tale to tell,
Where logic trips and laughs as well.

With beams of humor, all entwined,
Our thoughts embrace, hilariously blind.
Through tangled paths of wit we roam,
Finding wisdom's joyful home.

So join this mesh of playful prose,
Where understanding wears silly clothes.
In this lattice, let's embrace the fun,
And dance in joy until we're done!

Unseen Horizons

I took a trip to look around,
But every road just spun me 'round.
With maps that seem to mock my plight,
I ended up in Porky's Diner at night.

The waiter said, "What's your aim?"
I said, "To see—what's your name?"
He laughed and served me leafy greens,
And I should've asked for fries and beans.

I climbed a hill to catch the breeze,
But all I saw were buzzing bees.
I aimed for stars but found a bin,
For lost hopes and a broken tin.

So here I stand, my view quite clear,
With visions of pie and an ice-cold beer.
If it's adventure that you seek,
Just don't forget your favorite snack to sneak.

The Canvas of Exploration

I packed my bags for a grand sight,
But tripped on shoes, now isn't that right?
With paint on my face and ketchup stains,
I ventured forth through joyous lanes.

The guide said, "Trust your inner guide!"
But I chose the path where squirrels slide.
They pointed left, I took a chance,
And ended up in a critter dance.

With visions bright and laughter loud,
I painted the town, oh what a crowd!
A canvas smeared with unseen art,
Of funny faces that flirt with heart.

So here I roam in silly glee,
In a wonderland, not meant for me.
With brushes dipped in joy and cream,
My canvas buzzes—like a dream.

Kaleidoscope of Views

Through the glass I peer and squint,
With each new angle, different lint.
That chair's a dragon, that cat a queen,
What a sight—like I'm in a scene!

I turned my head, what do I spy?
A bird in glasses, oh my, oh my!
A tiny frog in a tuxedo suit,
Dancing about—who knew they'd hoot?

The walls are talking, they say, "Oh dear!"
Should we engage? Should we give a cheer?
Their jumbled words make no fine sense,
But hints of giggles in every tense.

So let me twirl through this delightful maze,
In a kaleidoscope that dares to graze.
Each view a chuckle, each glance a glee,
In this silly world, come dance with me!

Layers of Perception

Looking for depth in pancake stacks,
I found a treasure! Just some shacks.
With syrup rivers sweetly flow,
And waffle boats in a sticky show.

The chef wore socks of polka dots,
While flipping pancakes, misfired shots!
Each layer stacked with jokes and cheer,
In this breakfast land, I'm a pioneer.

Through narrow glimpses, I start to see,
That life is layered hilariously.
With a spritz of cream and a cherry on top,
I'll take a slide—plop, plop, plop!

So come explore this delightful plate,
Where nothing's dull, and laughs await.
With layers stacked like stories told,
Each perception sprinkles a bit of gold!

Canvased Wonders

In the midst of chaos, I see a scene,
A dog on a skateboard, oh what a glean.
With cats wearing hats, they dance with glee,
While squirrels compose, a nut symphony.

Paint splatters fly, like a wild balloon,
An elephant's trumpet, shaped like a spoon.
Amidst these oddities, laughter ignites,
In this wacky canvas, pure joy delights.

Each frame tells a tale, absurd yet grand,
While penguins juggle, under a sun so bland.
A bearded lady sings of pies in the sky,
While unicorns prance, quite close by.

So let's grab our brushes, and color the day,
With chuckles and giggles, in a quirky way.
Life's a masterpiece, let laughter unfold,
In this canvased wonder, let stories be told.

In Pursuit of Clarity

I squint through the fog, hoping to see,
A cat in a bow tie, sipping on tea.
The world is a circus, with funny little sights,
Like monkeys in tuxes, having grand fights.

I chase down the clues, but they slip and slide,
A fish wearing glasses, all filled with pride.
A sheep with a mustache, is reading a book,
In this quest for clarity, I'm hooked on the hook.

Each twist in my path brings a giggle and grin,
As turtles in top hats spin round in a din.
With a map drawn in chocolate, I'm led astray,
By a chicken that clucks, pointing the way.

So here's to the chase, and the laughter it brings,
To absurd little moments, and silly things.
Within this chaos, my heart finds light,
In pursuit of clarity, everything feels right.

Waves of Perspective

On the beach, I watch, a crab with a dream,
Dancing in sandals, it's quite the theme.
A seagull dressed smartly, with a top hat too,
Sipping on soda, in the ocean's blue.

Waves crash and whisper, secrets untold,
A fish wearing glasses, rather bold.
Surfboards on llamas, parade down the shore,
These waves of perspective, who could ask for more?

With each splash of laughter, the tide starts to swell,
A jellyfish jiving, it dances so well.
Clams cracking jokes, and barnacles sing,
In this whimsical water, joy is the king.

So, come ride the currents, let humor define,
The quirks of the ocean, are truly divine.
In every wave, a story awaits,
With laughter as foam, life elevates.

The Horizon Within

I gaze at the sky, where balloons take flight,
A rabbit in shades, says 'Isn't this bright?'
A parade of odd creatures, oh what a show,
With penguins on roller skates, moving so slow.

In this world of nonsense, I see strange things,
Like a bear with a ukulele, strumming sweet strings.
A fish on a bicycle, rides with such flair,
In the horizon within, there's magic to share.

The trees play tambourines, what a grand sound,
While flying pigs twirl, and dance round and round.
As the sun sets softly, painting the sky,
Laughter erupts, as the clouds drift by.

So here in my mind, where quirks are amiss,
Each thought is a treasure, just pure bliss.
In chasing the funny, I find a truth,
The horizon within, forever is youth.

Journey on a Distant Line

Riding on a train of dreams,
Chasing all the wildest schemes.
The candy man forgot his stash,
And now we're stuck with a piñata bash.

Each crinkle crackle, oh what a sound,
We dance and laugh, feeling quite unbound.
The sun sets low with cheeky grins,
As rabbits cheer for their Easter wins.

A squirrel in a tux drinks from a cup,
Everyone stops to cheer him up.
With popcorn clouds floating up high,
We wink and nod, oh my, oh my!

But as night falls with giggles galore,
We sip on clouds and beg for more.
This train ride's twisty, topsy-turvy,
With all things silly, never so nervy.

Light Between the Shadows

In the nooks where whispers play,
Lies a banana dreaming away.
He's dressed in pajamas, quite the sight,
Skipping shadows till the morning light.

The lamp post moon winks, oh so bright,
As squirrels dress in coats of white.
They strut around like tiny kings,
Oh, the joy that silly night brings!

A shadow cat with a crown of cheese,
Sings to the wind, doing just as he please.
While owls debate, with eyes so wide,
On whether to sleep or take a ride.

At dawn's arrival, all seems a dream,
Bananas and squirrels join in a team.
With laughter echoing, off the crops,
In this world, time never stops.

The Intersection of Thoughts

At the corner of whimsy and fun,
Lies a pizza, under a blazing sun.
Toppings tumble like thoughts in a whirl,
As everyone laughs at the pepperoni swirl.

A taco stands, with a bowtie neat,
Offering thoughts on mixed-up meat.
You'd think it's strange, this culinary fight,
But tacos dance while pizzas take flight!

The ketchup bottle clinks like a bell,
While mustard sings of a more yummy spell.
They plot and plan behind the scenes,
To turn this feast into wacky dreams.

As minds collide, flavors explode,
In this buffet of a thought highway road.
Where everything's kooky, and nothing's the same,
Let's all join in and play this strange game!

Timeless Gazes

In a park where clocks have no hands,
A turtle races, leaving funny strands.
The sun's a joker, hiding behind,
And giggling softly, as if so blind.

With pocket watches that giggle and tick,
Trees tell secrets with their own little tricks.
While squirrels mime in a timeless play,
Chasing owls who just want to sway.

Grasshoppers sing a tune so bold,
While frogs narrate tales of the old.
In this timeless place, jokes know no age,
As laughter flips open the funniest page.

So pass the hours with a wink and a smile,
In this silly park, stay for a while.
For time is a jester, wearing a mask,
And who needs minutes for fun? Just ask!

The Depth of Awareness

My cat thinks she's a queen, it's true,
She sits on my head, as I sip my brew.
I wonder if she knows my stress,
Or just enjoys her furry finesse.

Each time I search for a snack to munch,
I find a hairball, replacing my lunch.
My friends all laugh, 'It's a cat's domain!'
But who's the one cleanin' up the remain?

In the chaos of home, I find a few,
Socks in odd places, is this case anew?
Awareness grows like a wild-eyed hare,
As I sneak past the laundry with utmost care.

Infinity's Embrace

I spotted a toddler, just learning to walk,
His charming waddle, oh what a mock!
He trips on his shoes, lies down with a giggle,
Mom's photo-ready, as he starts to wiggle.

The dog in the park thinks he's quite the chap,
Chasing his tail, oh what a mishap!
Spinning in circles, a dizzying dance,
If only he'd stop, maybe he'd have a chance!

On swings of infinity, the laughter does swing,
As kids try to fly without any string.
Each glimpse of their joy makes me feel free,
In this crazy parade, so blissfully spree.

Capturing Fleeting Moments

A squirrel darted past with a nut in his beak,
It looked quite absurd, I couldn't help but peek.
He stopped for a moment, proud and aloof,
Then disappeared quick, like a thief on the roof.

I caught a glimpse of my neighbor's pet pig,
Wagging its tail, could it be any big?
It rolled in the grass, making quite a mess,
While the owner just sighed, "What did I guess?"

Moments slip by like a wink of a jive,
Before we can blink, they jump and arrive.
Snapshots in hearts, too quick to define,
Life's fleeting moments, oh how they shine!

Embracing Change in Sight

I found my old shoes, one's covered in dust,
Worn down from journeys, but who can I trust?
The laces are tangled, the soles quite askew,
Yet they still hold memories, oh yes, it's true!

The fridge door creaks, I peek inside for a snack,
An experiment's brewing or is that an attack?
Leftovers whisper, "Remember that night?"
When dinner was a gamble, what a fun fright!

Change comes in waves, like the tide at play,
From cats to old shoes, they linger and sway.
Embracing it all, with laughter and glee,
For life's funny dance, is where I want to be!

The Horizon of Ideas

In the distance, thoughts do roam,
Chasing dreams like a lost gnome.
Ideas pop like popcorn's fluff,
Each one warps our minds, quite tough.

Jokes fly high on a zephyr's wing,
Snapping branches with each zing.
We throw them high, watch them spin,
Draw a mustache on a squirrel's grin.

Every thought's a kite, set free,
Tangled in branches of a nearby tree.
The wind laughs as we try to reel,
Our silly whims are all too real.

So we gather, laughter loud and bright,
In this playful quest, oh what a sight!
With each idea, a world we can build,
It's all absurd, yet wholly thrilled.

Colors of Awareness

A rainbow sprinkles in your mind,
Where thoughts go wild and unwind.
Yellow giggles and blue takes a dive,
In this quirky realm, we're all alive.

Red stands up, waves a big hand,
While green thinks it's in a rock band.
Orange is painting without a care,
As purple dances in the square.

The colors splash, they twist and tease,
With bubblegum dreams and a sprinkle of breeze.
Fingers sticky, paint everywhere,
In a world that's more fun with an added flare.

So let's blend more and make a mess,
With laughter and cheer that we can express.
For in each hue, there's a grin to share,
Life's a colorful show, without a spare.

The Subtle Canvas

On a canvas, thoughts will blend,
Splatters of ideas, around the bend.
A brush strokes laughter where none has been,
Creating shapes from thin air, with a grin.

You might see a cat with a hat askew,
Twirling about in a lovely hue.
A fish with wings just took a bow,
In this quirky gallery, oh wow!

With every dash and every stroke,
The colors giggle, they speak and poke.
Who knew a canvas could be so witty?
Brushing off blunders, oh what a pity!

So grab some paint, let's have a blast,
With funny shapes that are sure to last.
In this palette of play, laughter swells,
Art is a joke that no one repels.

Beyond the Frame

Pictures dance outside their frame,
Jumping out, they play a game.
A dog with glasses reads a book,
While a cat in a suit gives a knowing look.

Twist and turn! The canvas shakes,
As drawn delights make silly breaks.
A clock with wings takes to the skies,
While laughter spills from our sleepy eyes.

Photos giggle, as moments leap,
Chasing butterflies in a playful sweep.
What lies beyond but a chuckle and cheer,
In this pixelated world we hold dear.

So let's break frames, let chaos reign,
In the art of life, let's entertain.
For beyond the frame is where we roam,
A gallery full of joy—we're home!

Boundless Vistas

In glasses thick, I scout the scene,
Where squirrels dodge like nimble dreams.
A kite flies by, twisted in flight,
I wave to it, the sky's delight.

A cow in stripes, what a sight!
Moo-ing loudly, day turns to night.
I ponder life with a frown,
While a chicken tries to strut around.

At sunset's glow, I trip on turf,
A tumble sends me headfirst, with mirth.
The world unfolds, so wild and broad,
Yet I find my face, it meets the sod!

Through all the quirks that life can show,
I laugh and smile, oh what a flow.
For every blunder in my spree,
Is just a new view made for me.

Reflections of the Soul

A pond so clear, no fish in sight,
I splash and see my laugh take flight.
A frog croaks back, how rude indeed!
He leaps away, I plant a seed.

With ducks in line, a feathered queue,
They seem to plan a day so blue.
I watch them wobble, oh what grace,
As one takes flight, I change my pace.

The sun reflects, a bright bouquet,
While I trip up on my own ballet.
I wave to birds, they laugh and tease,
Life's little quirks make me sneeze.

With every splash, a giggle bright,
The pond's my stage, who needs the fright?
In every ripple, a story told,
A soul that dances, brave and bold.

The Expansive Gaze

A mountain high, a perfect view,
Where yodeling goats make their debut.
They leap and bound, no care at all,
While I look on, ready to fall.

A hawk swoops low, my lunch it spies,
I shield my sandwich, hear my cries!
With every bite, I laugh, unsure,
That bird's a thief, of that I'm sure.

Near the edge, I tip and sway,
A tumble could lead me astray.
But here I stand, with fingers crossed,
For laughter, not fear, is never lost.

With every glance, a joke unfolds,
Nature's humor forever bold.
The world's a canvas, a goofy play,
And I'm just here to laugh and sway.

Echoes in the Distance

A shout to mountains, echoes bounce,
What was that? A whistle? A pounce?
A rabbit hops, pricks up its ear,
It seems we share a thrill of cheer.

Beyond the hills, a tour bus roars,
With tourists lost, they seek the shores.
I wave them in, what sights they'll see,
Once they find their way, just let them be!

The wind carries giggles, the trees sway along,
Each rustle a chord in nature's song.
I dance with the shadows, a skipping spree,
While critters join in, as wild as can be.

With each echo, life brings a jest,
A chance to laugh, no need for rest.
In this vast expanse, the fun never ends,
With every glance, on laughter depends.

A Synthesis of Views

In a land where glasses grow,
Each pair tells a joke, you know.
One is up, the other down,
Sight's a circus in this town.

Optics dance, they twist and spin,
A lensy laugh beneath my chin.
Voices echo, and then they clash,
My left eye grins while my right eye dashes.

Reality is a playful maze,
Through these frames, I'm lost for days.
A whimsical world where lines will bend,
Every glance, a laughing friend.

So come and join this sightful spree,
Bring along your wobbly glee.
For every blunder and curious peek,
Life's a joke, and vision's chic!

Bridges of Perspective

Two planks swaying in the breeze,
Pondering life with utmost ease.
One side says, "Jump and see!"
The other shouts, "Better not, that's me!"

Wobbly legs support our chat,
Views colliding in a spinny spat.
Each step we take, a sight surprise,
Chuckle at the lows and highs.

Wide and far the laughter flows,
Overlooking pitfalls and muddy throes.
One eye squinty, the other wide,
Balance beams of the bright-eyed tide.

So let's gather and share a view,
A bridge of laughs, a frame or two.
Here's to perspectives packing fun,
Life's strange, but we're never done!

The Uncharted Vision

Through a lens that's yet to clear,
I spy a squirrel that sounds like a deer.
With every blink, a mystery formed,\nUnfocused worlds where humor's warmed.

Maps are drawn in playful doodle,
In a land where all things noodle.
The sky's a floor, the grass, a wall,
Here every trip will make you fall.

Navigating through a laugh or two,
I wink at clouds and say, "How do you?"
Lost in this comic escapade,
Between sight and silliness, I wade.

A journey crafted with quirky sights,
Fumbling through delightful flights.
Adventure calls without direction,
Each chuckle leads to fresh affection!

Whirlwind of Reflections

Round and round the mirrors spin,
Chasing laughter tucked within.
A little twist, a funny face,
Reality's a goofy race.

Reflections wink, they toss and tease,
With every blink, the brain gets squeezed.
I look left, and there's a clown,
Giggles echo all through the town.

In this whirlwind, sights go wild,
Every glance, a friendly child.
Jokes collide in a laugh parade,
Where every vision is homemade.

So grab a friend, and join the fun,
Under the rays of a glowing sun.
In this carousel of blurry dreams,
We'll find out how funny vision seems!

Landscape of Beliefs

In my mind's vast plains they roam,
Ideas sprout like wildflowers grown.
Some are bright, others plain as toast,
I water dreams, they flourish most.

Skeptic goats graze on the doubts,
While bunnies hop around the shouts.
I paint my thoughts in colors bright,
Each brushstroke brings a new delight.

Frilly clouds float above my head,
Whispers from them fill me with dread.
They say to dream with all your might,
But watch for bugs, they bite quite right!

As I stroll through this wacky land,
I trip on truth, it's quite unplanned.
The grass giggles; I chuckle too,
In this landscape, who needs the blues?

The Scenery of Growth

I planted seeds of silly schemes,
Watered them with laughter streams.
From tiny sprouts, they grew so wide,
Now they dance, I can't abide!

The carrots laugh when I can't see,
They jump around and tease me, whee!
Tomatoes blush and hide away,
They say it's all a game we play.

In this garden, weeds wear crowns,
While daisies spin and knock us down.
Fungi with hats conduct a show,
As plants all groove, they steal the glow!

With each new bloom, my heart takes flight,
Who knew growth could feel so light?
I'll dance with weeds, we'll paint the town,
In this great garden, I wear the crown!

A Dance of Dimensions

In a world where socks go missing,
I found a party worth dismissing.
Between the folds of space and time,
I tripped on thoughts, oh what a climb!

The clocks are waltzing side to side,
While shadows dance, they never hide.
Quadrants giggle, points do sway,
Laughing at angles lost at play.

Round and round, the circles spin,
Inviting all, no one stays in.
Dimensions twist like two left feet,
In this jig, there's no defeat!

As I shuffle through this cosmic ball,
I trip on truths that rise and fall.
With a wink, I signal the stars,
In this dance, we'll cross the bars!

Beyond the Veil

What lies beyond the curtain's sway?
A land of jokes on full display.
Where whispers tickle, giggles soar,
And adventures knock upon the door.

Beneath this veil, a comical crew,
Puppets dance, and shadows woo.
They plot and scheme, oh what a sight,
Each silliness blooms in pure delight!

A cantaloupe sings karaoke here,
While broccoli strums a pint-sized leer.
The scene is wild, the laughter spread,
As nonsense reigns, the sane seem dead.

With each reveal, the chuckles grow,
Beyond the veil, there's always a show.
So lift that drape, come take a peek,
Where hilarity thrives, and fun's unique!

Fragments of Light

In the corner of my eye, a sight,
A cat wearing glasses, what a delight.
Chasing shadows, but oh, what a fuss,
Losing the battle, it's just too much.

Squirrels with acorns, plotting their schemes,
Under the tree, it's more than it seems.
They wave tiny flags, what a parade,
Making a mess of their crunchy crusade.

A dog with a hat, prancing with flair,
Struts down the sidewalk, stops to stare.
With sunglasses on and a wagging tail,
He thinks he's the captain, but oh, how he'll fail.

The sunbeams dance, in a jolly way,
Making shadows do the salsa ballet.
While I trip over my own two shoes,
And laugh at my luck, it's all so amused.

Pathways of Awareness

Walking the path where grass is tall,
I spot a frog with a monocle, standing small.
He gives me a nod, and I giggle aloud,
As he jumps in a puddle, proud and unbowed.

Around the bend, there's a squirrel on wheels,
Riding a skateboard, oh, what a squeal!
He flips in the air, a daring stunt,
But lands in the leaves with a rather loud grunt.

A duck with a briefcase, dressed in a tie,
Quacks about deadlines, oh my, oh my!
As pigeons in suits hold a meeting near,
With plans for their coops, the end is quite clear.

Hilarity blooms in this bright, wild space,
Where antics unfold with such playful grace.
The world seems bigger in moments of fun,
And each little giggle is surely well-won.

Echoes in the Distance

I hear a loud honk from the sky above,
Two geese in tuxedos, well, isn't that love?
As they argue over who's in charge today,
The honking is music but funny in play.

An owl with a clipboard checks off his list,
Counting the stars — oh, look at the twist!
He trips on a branch, feathers everywhere,
And chuckles at how he really doesn't care.

Beneath a blue sky, a parade of ants,
Marching in formation, they look for romance.
With tiny red flowers and a grand little song,
They dance to the rhythm, where could they belong?

In each little moment, the laughter persists,
Life's little wonders, we can't help but insist.
Echoes of joy fill this curious space,
Reminding us all to keep up the chase.

Luminescent Horizons

At twilight, the lights begin to twinkle,
A firefly party makes my thoughts crinkle.
They flash their bulbs like disco lights,
Inviting the stars to join in their sights.

A goat on a roof, with glasses and flair,
Waves to the moon in the cool evening air.
He's hosting a dance for all critters galore,
With beats that would make even wolves roar.

Under the glow of this luminous scene,
A raccoon with a guitar serenades the green.
His songs of the night, they echo and bounce,
And even the crickets join in for a pounce.

In these whimsical moments, laughter takes flight,
The world full of wonders, all shining so bright.
With joy all around, we dance till the dawn,
In this world of delight, we're never forlorn.

Through the Lens of Wonder

I bought a pair of glasses, quite a sight,
They let me see the world in a mood so bright.
I asked my cat what she thought of the view,
She yawned and said, "I just see more of you."

With every little giggle, I scratch my head,
Is that a butterfly or my neighbor's shed?
Through lenses frosted with a sprinkle of cheer,
I peek at the mundane, and it all feels queer.

There's magic in the oddest things I find,
Like socks that vanish, oh, were they ever kind?
And my dog wears shades, thinking he's so bold,
But really, it's just to keep the sun controlled.

So here's to seeing life through silly frames,
Where every silly moment ignites new games.
With laughter in focus, the world spins around,
In this goofy realm, joy is tightly bound.

Whispers of the Unseen

In the corner of my eye, shadows play peek-a-boo,
Are they ghosts of snack time, or just dust in the view?
I chase after whispers, thoughts dancing like flies,
Swatting at memories, what a cheeky surprise!

There's a sock monster lurking beneath my bed,
I swear it's plotting to take my shoes instead.
I caught a glimpse of the fridge's bright glow,
It winked at me slyly, offering leftovers to stow.

The plants in my garden gossip, so I've heard,
"Who needs sunny weather? It's the worms that get stirred!"
And bees have a secret, buzzing with glee,
Should I ask for their wisdom or just let them be?

With sights that are hidden, my heart skips a beat,
For every new angle, life's a whimsical treat.
In this realm of the unseen, laughter rings true,
A playful reminder that joy's always in view.

In the Eye of Insight

Look close, there's a donut, right there in the sky,
I might be delusional or just really high.
But oh, sweet temptation, if only it rained,
Frosting and sprinkles, my taste buds unexplained.

Am I seeing things clearly, or is it a glitch?
My neighbor's waving, is he throwing a pitch?
With goggles of laughter, the world looks absurd,
I grin like a fool, as I stare at a bird.

Life's wisdom is funky; it tickles and bites,
Like socks that get lost or a shadow that fights.
It's not what you see, but the laugh that you make,
'Cause even the serious need a good cake break.

Wobbling through moments, I cherish each goof,
Finding joy in the madness, I dance on the roof.
With insight that's playful, life's mishaps are gold,
In the eye of the funny, the universe unfolds.

The Mosaic of Experience

Collecting odd stories, I'm curators of quirks,
Like that time at the party, I danced in my jerks.
The pieces are funky, mismatched tiles in play,
But oh, how they shine in their silly ballet!

From old ladies knitting to toddlers who scream,
My world is a patchwork, a whimsical dream.
Each laugh is a fragment, a smirk sewn with care,
Stitching moments of joy with an accidental flair.

I found a lost sandwich, it whispered to me,
"Don't worry, dear friend, I still hope to be free!"
A mosaic of humor, bright colors combine,
Creating a canvas of absurd, and divine.

So here's to our journeys, a fun, hoppy ride,
With each little adventure and giggle inside.
In this patchwork of life, let's gather and cheer,
For the whimsy we uncover, year after year.

Realm of Possibilities

In a world where cows wear shoes,
And chickens play the blues,
The sky's a friend, with clouds to share,
A jam session up in the air.

Flip-flops dance upon the grass,
As rabbits hop, they take a pass;
A picnic spread with jelly beans,
Among the wildest of daydreams.

Squirrels in hats, they strut with glee,
As laughter blooms like flowers free;
Who knew this place could be so wild?
Imagination, nature's child!

So come along, don't be too shy,
Where elephants learn how to fly;
In this realm, your thoughts can soar,
Leave your shoes right by the door!

The Sightline of Hope

In a world where socks don't match,
And every thought's a quirky catch;
A lizard tells jokes, quite absurd,
While turtles hum a silly word.

A unicorn and a moose take tea,
Discussing the latest meme you see;
The flowers giggle, they sway and twirl,
As silly thoughts begin to whirl.

Clouds wear hats, they're quite the flair,
With donut holes in the air;
Chasing sunshine, they burst with glee,
In this line of laughter, come have a spree!

Join the dance, let go of frowns,
Where every smile unfurls the crowns;
Together, let's weave this brilliant scope,
In the sightline of all our hope!

Chasing the Invisible

A ghost with a laugh plays peek-a-boo,
With ice cream cones and a kitty too;
They race through fields of socks and bows,
Chasing dreams where secret joy grows.

Invisible cars zoom by with flair,
While polka-dot frogs do a silly dare;
Together they skip, they leap, they jump,
In a world that's full of giggle and thump.

The moon winks down with a cheeky glance,
Inviting all stars to join the dance;
With every step, the laughter rises,
Chasing the fun brings endless surprises!

So hop along with the giggling mad,
In this chase, you'll never be sad;
With invisible friends, we'll race the night,
Chasing the unseen, oh what a sight!

Invisible Roads to Discovery

There's a path in soup where the spoon won't stir,
And the carrots dance, oh what a blur;
Invisible roads where giggles compile,
A map made of dreams goes mile by mile.

Butterflies wear coats, striped and bright,
With cupcakes spinning through day and night;
They share their secrets, soft and sweet,
On paths of sprinkles, a tasty feat.

In a land where jellybeans rain from the sky,
The invisible roads go all awry;
Join the adventure, let's wander and play,
Discovering magic in our own funny way!

So grab a fried egg and a sock that talks,
As we chase the unseen with hopping socks;
These roads of laughter, so silly and bright,
Lead to discoveries that tickle delight!

Lenses of the Heart

Through rose-tinted specs, we see it all,
A cat in a hat, wearing fish for a shawl.
Love's blind angle gives us quite a show,
As we giggle at tripping on toes that we know.

With a squint and a grin, we catch every glance,
A clown on a trampoline, performing a dance.
In this wacky world of distorted delight,
We toast with our cups and laugh through the night.

Each flutter of lashes, a twist of the fate,
Our hearts do a jig, and it's never too late.
We peer through the laughter; we squawk and we squeal,
In this circus of feelings, it's all quite surreal.

So wear your bright goggles, they make you look smart,
Through a lens full of love, we'll never fall apart.
With a skip and a hop, let's play our part right,
In this carnival of joy, let's dance in the light!

In the Realm of the Unexplored

Explore the odd paths where penguins wear shoes,
And cats ponder life while sipping their brews.
With maps made of laughter and compasses too,
We voyage through madness, just me and you.

In jungles of jellybeans, wild monkeys swing,
A cacophony of giggles that the sparrows all bring.
We chase down the rainbows, with socks on our heads,
Inventing more whimsies, ignoring the threads.

With each curious turn, new puzzles unfold,
Like fish that tell stories and berries so bold.
We'll find treasure in hiccups, and joy in a frown,
In antics of clowns, we can never wear down.

So raise up your flippers, pretend you can fly,
In this realm of the unknown, we were born to try.
With whimsy our guide, let's laugh as we roam,
In the land of the silly, we'll always feel home!

Shadows of Understanding

In shadows we wander, with ice cream in hand,
We trip over giggles, and yes, that was planned.
Quirky conundrums dance in our sight,
As we laugh at the chaos until the sunlight.

With each silly shadow that jigs on the wall,
We ponder the meaning of one silly fall.
Like ducks wearing sunglasses, so chic and so bright,
We chase all our worries and embrace what feels right.

Underneath the moonlight, mischief does bloom,
Laughter echoes softly, pushing away gloom.
In this waltz of confusion, we find our own way,
With shadows our partners, we laugh through the day.

From hiccups of wisdom to blunders so grand,
We tiptoe on giggles, as we make our own band.
In a riddle of chuckles, understanding is found,
Through shadows of laughter, our hearts are unbound!

Breath of the Cosmos

With cosmic balloons that float in the air,
We giggle at stardust stuck in our hair.
Silly little aliens join in the fun,
Playing games of tag beneath the bright sun.

From moons made of marshmallows to stars dressed in spark,
We spin through the universe, making our mark.
A nebula of laughter swirls brightly around,
As we leap through the galaxies, joy knows no bounds.

In the whimsy of planets, we kick up a fuss,
While creatures of wonder board our crazy bus.
With space cakes and smiles, we toast to the night,
In this vast, silly cosmos, everything's bright.

So grab your antenna, let's dance like the wind,
With the breath of the cosmos, our spirits unpinned.
We'll giggle with comets, take joy in the ride,
In this hilarious universe, let's laugh side by side!

Landscapes of the Mind

A cow in a tutu dances with glee,
While cacti do pirouettes, wild and free.
The trees wear glasses, oh what a sight,
And squirrels debate who's really the bright.

Clouds float by, gossiping like old friends,
As raindrops join in, their laughter transcends.
The mountains are tickled by a mischievous breeze,
While rivers giggle, teasing the bees.

Where Dreams Unfold

Puppies in capes fly over the moon,
While pancakes dance, singing a tune.
A cat makes toast with a flick of its paw,
And fish in bow ties are the latest awe.

Balloons hold meetings, discussing their fate,
While carrots debate if they're vegetables or bait.
A sandwich juggernaut runs down the street,
And pickles roll by with a jazzy beat.

Crystalline Views

The ice cream truck sings, but it's out of tune,
While jellybeans argue who's favorite to shoo.
A waffle in glasses reads poetry loud,
And a teapot is crowned, summoning a crowd.

Snowmen in sunglasses sip lemonade,
While marshmallows gossip in the shade.
A skateboard-riding carrot steals the show,
And fruit flies become the stars of the flow.

Eyes Wide Open

Giraffes wear hats that are tall as can be,
While turtles sing ballads under a tree.
A raccoon writes novels, all clever and spry,
And donut-shaped clouds drift lazily by.

With eyes wide open, the world is absurd,
As squirrels campaign to be mayor, unheard.
Pumpkins juggle at the county fair,
While ghosts and goblins play tag in the air.

Eyes Like Open Windows

My eyes are like windows, wide and keen,
They watch the antics of the unseen.
A fly on the wall plays a sneaky game,
I laugh so hard, I forget its name.

Squirrels plotting, as if they know,
Which nuts to hide, and where to go.
They wink at me, I chuckle back,
In their mad world, I'm never on track.

The radar of my sight sees odd motions,
My neighbor's dog making wild ocean commotions.
With each strange act, the humor grows,
The everyday life, a silly show.

Through these windows, terrific sights,
A cat on a skateboard, oh what delights!
I giggle as the world spins 'round,
In this grand circus, joy is found.

Tapestry of Sight

In the tapestry of what I can see,
There's a jester juggling with a bumblebee.
The sun is a spotlight, shining so bright,
On a duck wearing sunglasses, quite a sight!

Each thread in my gaze, colored by hue,
A dog wearing slippers, who knew it could do?
The garden is laughing, flowers all swaying,
Bees buzz along, like they're DJing.

A picnic unfolds with ants in a line,
Dinner for them, oh isn't it fine?
I can't help but giggle, can't hold it in,
As they struggle with crumbs, their mission a win.

In this patchwork of chuckles, I find my delight,
Observing these moments makes everything bright.
With every glance, a new funny score,
My tapestry's woven with joy evermore.

A Landscape of Thoughts

My thoughts stretch out as a silly view,
A cow plays chess, beats a pig at a duel.
The trees whisper jokes, they crack me up,
While rabbits sip tea in a dainty cup.

Mountains of laughter, valleys of cheer,
Every quirky thought that brings me near.
Clouds bubble and twist, in laughter they roll,
A landscape of fun, that tickles the soul.

Fish on bicycles, what a strange show,
Riding through puddles, with nowhere to go.
Each ripple of chuckles spreads far and wide,
In this vast landscape, I thrive with pride.

So while I wander this humorous land,
With giggles and quirks, I take a firm stand.
My thoughts' panorama, forever in bloom,
Turns the world bright with laughter and zoom!

Beyond the Gaze

What lies beyond the normal sight,
Is a cat who believes it can take flight.
With wings made of dreams, it leaps with a cheer,
Every tumble of fur brings more laughter near.

The sun is a cheeky prankster today,
Warming the snowmen who melt and sway.
They throw tiny snowballs in joyous surprise,
As I watch this nonsense, I can't help but rise.

Up above, the birds are busy rehearsing,
A musical number that's truly dispersing.
They chirp out a tune that tickle my laugh,
Their concert so silly, it's scored by a calf.

Beyond every gaze, the absurd awaits,
Where humor finds homes in the quirkiest traits.
With a wink or a nod to the scenes that unfold,
Life's comedy shines, forever untold.

Horizon's Embrace

Look at that cow with a curious stare,
Winking at birds in a casual flare.
The sun dances low, a bright golden ball,
As rabbits play tag through the tall, green hall.

A hat on a scarecrow, quite out of place,
Wind tickles daisies, they giggle with grace.
A farmer trips over his own muddy boots,
Chasing his chickens, they're picking their hoots.

A kite in the sky with a playful twist,
Swirling with clouds, it can't be missed.
Butterflies laugh as they flit through the air,
While ants have a meeting, none of them care.

Silly old tractor rolls past with a grin,
Every bump in the road makes it laugh with a spin.
The horizon is bright, filled with fun and delight,
With sights that bring smiles from morning to night.

Sight Beyond the Veil

Behind the curtain, a comedy show,
Squirrels wear glasses, putting on a glow.
A raccoon with popcorn, enjoying the view,
While mice play charades, just a few in the crew.

The fruit flies debate if bananas are prime,
While a snail sets a record for climbing in time.
A hedgehog in tights twirls around with finesse,
He tumbles and rolls; Oh, what a mess!

A butterfly whispers the gossip of dusk,
"Did you see that old bee? He's lost all his buzz!"
The leaves are all giggling, sharing a tease,
As fireflies chuckle, swaying with ease.

So lift the veil, let laughter abound,
In the hidden world where joy can be found.
With whimsical moments beneath a bright veil,
Life's a grand stage, go on and hit the trail!

The Art of Perception

A potato wearing shades, what a sight!
He thinks he's the star of the vegetable night.
On the radio, beets sing a tune,
While carrots in tuxes waltz under the moon.

A clever old onion tries to act bold,
But when he takes center stage, he starts to unfold.
With tears in the crowd, the laughter erupts,
As peas roll around, forming friendship in cups.

The art of perspective, a funny little dance,
Where a vine's got a dream of a grand romance.
The squash tells a tale of a pumpkin who grew,
Into a giant with dreams — can you believe it's true?

With patterns of joy, like a patchwork quilt,
The garden's alive with laughter it built.
In the end, it's the humor that brings us together,
In the art of perception, life's light as a feather!

Gaze Into the Infinite

In the deep green meadow, a goat plays the flute,
He thinks he's a legend, a very cool brute.
While sheep charge their phones, all busy and bright,
As butterflies log in to check their sweet flight.

A wise old owl wearing a monocle high,
Judges a contest of who can soar high.
With dreams of a world where the worms hold a race,
The grass sways and giggles, keeping up with the pace.

A cat with a cap claims he's seen it all,
From the birds in the sky to the ants at the mall.
He flips through the pages of whimsical lore,
While frogs in tuxedos. They just want to soar!

So gaze into the depths, where the silly take flight,
Where the improbable dances beneath stars so bright.
In a universe quirky, laughter's the key,
To unlock all the wonders of what we can see!

Envisioning Possibilities

In my backyard, a cat can fly,
A leap like magic, oh my, oh my!
Chasing dreams across the lawn,
Sipping tea with a fairy at dawn.

While squirrels debate the best cheese,
And ducks in tuxedos strut with ease.
I ponder wonders in the air,
With my slippers floating, what a pair!

Unicorns shopping right next door,
Choosing carrots; who could ask for more?
The sun is a toast, the moon a slice,
Peanut butter rain, oh so nice!

Every day's a riddle, it's true,
With weird reflections and colors askew.
In a world where giggles hold so much sway,
I dance in this merry place, hooray!

The Spectrum of Reality

In a world where socks can talk aloud,
They confabulate, so very proud.
My shoes wear hats, a sight to see,
As they dance around with glee!

Jellybeans rain from the skies above,
While pizza flies, a labor of love.
The clock sings tunes, oh, what a sound,
Tick-tock in harmony, spinning round!

Pigs on skateboards zip down the lane,
Each quack of a duck brings a chuckle in vain.
With colored glasses, I peek and pout,
Revealing hues I can't live without.

Reality winks with a sly little grin,
As I'm wrapped in laughter, losing my chin.
The ordinary twists, a colorful mix,
In this kaleidoscope, I find my fix!

Journeys Within the Mind

I sailed on thoughts, a paper boat,
Past jellyfish clouds, like dreams afloat.
In my head, a circus always plays,
With monkeys juggling for days and days.

Chasing ideas through cotton candy hills,
Where laughter bubbles and fun distills.
Invisible ropes tie us all in knots,
We giggle at secrets, oh, the plots!

A wizard's hat made of fried egg yolk,
Magic pours out with every joke.
I twirl through fantasies, wild and bright,
As mimes mime-glide in the warm sunlight.

So let's ride a wave of hilarious mirth,
Discovering treasure in each hearty birth.
In the caverns of whimsy, under the sun,
Adventures unravel, oh, what fun!

Finding Clarity in Chaos

When socks go missing in the laundry's spin,
Are they off to join a dance, or just sulking within?
The toaster confesses a craving for toast,
While the fridge hosts a party, that's no boring ghost!

Amidst the ruckus, a vision breaks free,
As rubber ducks chant in harmonic glee.
With licorice trees swaying in naught,
Chaos reveals what was never sought.

A blender's serenade, beats for the night,
As shadows tango with sheer delight.
Finding sense in the giggle and whirl,
Every calamity's a dance, a twirl!

So here's to the mayhem, the fun it brings,
To lost socks and talking things!
In this crazy carnival, clear and bright,
We dance in the chaos, a marvelous sight!

Through the Prism of Thought

In the mind's eye, a sight so bright,
Thoughts dance like stars, a comical flight.
I wonder if cows wear glasses for fun,
Or do they just stare at the clouds and run?

A flurry of dreams, like socks on a line,
They twist and they turn, completely benign.
Do fish ever ponder what lies in their bowl?
Or just wiggle about, their thoughts on a scroll?

Each thought is a bubble, some pop with a laugh,
Like a mind full of glitter, a child's photograph.
What if the moon took a selfie one night?
A glowing big cheese, that would be a sight!

So here's to the musings that twist in the breeze,
Like an umbrella caught in a cacophony of trees.
May our visions be silly, our laughter ignite,
In the prism of chaos, let's bask in delight!

Vistas of the Unseen

Hidden from view, yet right out of sight,
A nose in a book, but my cat takes a bite.
What's lurking behind that old coat on the chair?
A monster with manners? I'd like to declare!

Peeking through curtains with eyes big and round,
Squirrels in suits having meetings profound.
Why don't they join us for tea on the lawn?
I bet they'd sing songs until the break of dawn!

The world's full of quirks, like a jester's parade,
Invisible magic where all norms are swayed.
The styling of ants in their ballet of toil,
Perhaps they're just dancing from all that they spoil!

With shadows that prance and whispers that tease,
Embrace every giggle, find joy in the breeze.
Let laughter unveil what's unseen but clear,
In the playful dimensions, let's cheer and revere!

Reflections Beyond Boundaries

Mirrors that giggle twist truth on its head,
They whisper of kittens and cakes made of bread.
What if reflections just wanted to play?
Would they switch places? A delightful cliché!

Beyond every border, a riddle unfolds,
Like socks that wander, defying the molds.
What would a tree say if it could talk back?
I'd wager it's filled with tales of the wack!

The puddles of laughter, they ripple and shine,
Drawing circles of secrets in colors divine.
Do rainbows get tired of arching with grace?
Or just overthink how to show off their face?

Let's capture the giggles that dance in the air,
With imagination stretched like a bear in a chair.
In every reflection, may joy find its quest,
A universe bubbly, oh, laughter be blessed!

A Tapestry of Focus

Threads woven with humor, a tapestry grand,
Knitting together the quirks by demand.
Do you think clouds gossip about sunburned birds?
Or trade silly stories in whispers and words?

A patchwork of visions, a circus of sights,
Where jellybeans joust in ridiculous fights.
What if the grass just wanted to giggle?
Underfoot ballet turning each step into wiggle!

In this cloak of confusion, there's art everywhere,
With heckling hedgehogs and owls with flair.
Maybe a snail's wisdom is echoing slow,
Or a squirrel's quick charm has stolen the show!

So pull on your laughter, your giggles, your cheer,
In the fabric of life, let's dance without fear.
May our moments be vibrant, our joy be unbound,
In this tapestry woven, let silliness abound!

www.ingramcontent.com/pod-product-compliance
Lightning Source LLC
Chambersburg PA
CBHW051629160426
43209CB00004B/569